ISBN-10: 1515123413
ISBN-13: 978-1515123415

Printed in the United States
Amazon Create Space

Where There's a Wheel, There's a Way

Written By Kyle Pease and Todd Civin
Illustrations by Jason Boucher

Dedication

To say I would like to dedicate this book is an understatement. I would like to thank all of my family, all of my friends and my wonderful support team for always reminding me what it means to live by the motto, *Where There is a Wheel, There is a Way.*

Without your constant love, dedication and faith, none of this would be possible. So sit back and enjoy.

Where There Is a Wheel, There is a Way!!

-Kyle "Kpeasey" Pease

Never in my wildest dreams though believing that I can,
Did I think I'd hear the announcer say, "Kyle Pease, you're an Ironman."

There are very few who've earned this claim of all athletes on the earth,
And of those few, a very few were disabled at their birth.

140 plus point 6 miles is challenging as can be,
Even with strong arms and legs and not for guys like me.

My spirit and will are strong enough to make the finish mine,
But my body leaves me unequipped to toe the starting line.

With a strong push from my brother Brent, always there to save the day,
We proudly spread our message, "Where There's a Wheel, There Is a Way!"

With each struggle, a solution, as difficult as things may seem,
Brent's the legs and I'm the heart of the Pease's Racing Team.

3

My life was filled with stumbling blocks from the day that it began,
I lived each day as an Iron boy before becoming an Ironman.

Born at a local hospital as the second half of twins,
Raced my brother to the starting line, by two minutes Evan wins.

4

Though life began on slippery ground, from experience I will gain,
Caused by a lack of oxygen bringing damage to my brain.

My parents sensed there was something wrong, not acting like other boys.
I wasn't reaching milestones, rolling over or grasping toys.

They were saddened by the doctor's words, "Cerebral Palsy known as CP",
Agreed to include me just the same in each activity.

We always tried to focus on the things that I could do,
Though I may have done them differently, my failures there were few.

CP affects my arms and legs and impacts how I speak,
With no damage to my intelligence or the knowledge that I seek.

I reached the age to start in school and there was really no confusion,
I'd attend a school like everyone, teach the lessons of inclusion.

I experience life from a wheel chair instead of on two feet.
I took the bus each morning with my chair assigned a seat.

I approached each challenge differently, but was treated just the same.
The teachers knew I tried so hard and each kid learned my name.

Liked reading, spelling, art and math, learned each letter made a sound.
Loved to join the other kids when playtime came around.

I had an aide beside me who helped me in each class,
She'd take my notes and write for me, cut my food and hold my glass.

I know my strengths and weaknesses and at what things I'll succeed,
I accept my disability and that's the life I lead.

I may not win a foot race or a contest where I'd sing,
When asked if I would trade my life I wouldn't change a thing.

Assisted ball and track and field; best player that you'll meet,
This helped to set my future to become a triathlete.

Became the girl's hoop manager, as funny as it may seem,
Passed out towels and drinking water; the one guy on the team.

We all have disabilities, mine visible by my chair,
My parents knew I'd go to college, no excuse they'd want to hear.

I learned to live independently; a graduate of Kennesaw State,
Majored in Sports Management and this would be my fate.

Friends and family came to see me as the school announced my name,
They stood and cheered and yelled to me; I've never felt the same.

I'll remember that day forever; I still cannot believe it,
No matter how high the mountain, if you climb, you can achieve it.

I now had a diploma to hang upon the wall,
Could contribute to society when employers came to call.

My first job didn't pay much, was just a volunteer,
But I joined the work force anyway in the field of children's care.

14

I'm now employed at Publix where customers know my smile,
I greet them as they come to shop and lead them to each aisle.

I work at a local hospital; a greeter in patient relations,
I share my upbeat view of life when they're in for operations.

Despite all of my victories and following of life's guidelines,
I watched as Brent competed while I sat upon the sidelines.

When Brent became an Ironman and captured all the glory,
I hoped somehow to get involved and here I changed my story.

I cheered for Brent through every mile; I'd never be a hater,
I'll always be his biggest fan, but wished for something greater.

Following Ironman Louisville we both sat down to dinner,
I asked him how to get involved and make Team Pease a winner.

17

First race was the Charles Harris, a 10K like no other,
It wasn't about our finish time, but racing with my brother.

We competed in the Publix Half; feet never touched the ground,
My brother pushed all 13.1, the crowd cheered all around.

And then our first triathlon; Evan, Brent and I combined,
Evan ran, we biked and swam in a kayak right behind.

Each time we ran together, we saw our speed improve,
The more that I'd inspire Brent, the faster that we'd move.

19

To share this joyful feeling, when we heard each loud ovation,
We longed to give this thrill to others so we started our Foundation.

The Kyle Pease Foundation began with all humility,
Allowed others to participate despite their disability.

We've grown from two to twenty-two with countless volunteers,
Who spread KPF's mission of pushing athletes in chairs.

Our yearly bowling fundraiser and the Jake Vinson Family Grant,
Send kids to Camp Wheel-A-Way where there's no such word as can't.

We traveled to Wisconsin to become an Ironman,
Saw the challenge ahead of us but never doubted that we can.

Again in Panama City with wind blowing in our face,
We again were crowned as Ironman, it's like no other race.

Even being two-time Ironman with this feeling of elation,
Our victories aren't about Brent and me, but only the foundation.

Sharing a sense of accomplishment with the disabled population.
And to see the smiles on each face during victory celebration.

If I could change one thing in life, though I'd continue to compete,
I'd want to cross the finish line, not on wheels, but on two feet.

Still hoping that this dream occurs, and on that glorious day,
I'll change the name of my children's book to "Where There's Two Feet, There's a Way".

Together
We
Wheel!

The Kyle Pease Foundation

The purpose of the Kyle Pease Foundation (KPF) is to create awareness and raise funds to promote success for persons with disabilities by providing assistance to meet their individual needs through sports.

Programs may include scholarship opportunities, purchasing of medical equipment or adaptive sports equipment for others or contributing to other organizations that provide similar assistance to disabled persons as well as participating in educational campaigns to create awareness about Cerebral Palsy and other disabilities.

KPF will provide these services directly to individuals as well as to partner with other existing non-profit organizations to achieve these goals.

Direct benefits will be limited to persons with disabilities who need adaptive sports equipment, mobility devices or medical care.

Walking with KPeasey

Walking with KPeasey is a campaign affiliated with The Kyle Pease Foundation, Inc. (KPF). Walking with KPeasey works to create awareness and raise funds in support of KPF.

The Kyle Pease Foundation, in turn, promotes success for young persons with disabilities by providing assistance to meet their individual needs through sports and competition. Programs include scholarship opportunities, purchasing adaptive sports equipment, and participating in educational campaigns around Cerebral Palsy.

For more information, visit www.kylepeasefoundation.org.

About Kyle Pease

At Kennesaw State University, Kyle excelled in the Sports Management field. He worked on designing disabled athlete friendly sports facilities in Acworth, GA before graduating in 2008 with a BS in Sports Management. Throughout his time at KSU, he was an active member and event coordinator for ABLE (Advocacy, Boldness, Leadership, and Empowerment), KSU's disabled student organization. Kyle was also a brother of KSU's Pi Kappa Phi fraternity. Kyle has worked as a liaison and an ambassador at a major grocery store chain and at Children's Healthcare of Atlanta.

Kyle enjoys competing in marathons and Ironman races with his older brother, Brent. With the mission of instilling hope and determination, Kyle wants to help people see the world from a different view. Through his accomplishments and speeches he hopes to provide a positive outlook and inspiration for individuals looking for motivation in their own lives. Kyle's message, though always delivered with a sense of humor, is heartfelt and inspired by his unique perspective of life.

Kyle currently holds four down four jobs as well as running The Kyle Pease Foundation. As his motto goes "Together We Wheel" has become his personal mantra as well.

About Brent Pease

Brent, an avid sports fan, always enjoyed competing in sports as a child. It wasn't until he completed his first Iron-distance race in 2010 that he and Kyle really enjoyed sports together. Since then he has gone on to complete six Ironman races and numerous 70.3 & Olympic distance races. Brent swam at Woodward Academy and graduated from Florida State University. Brent is multi-sport coach with Dynamo Multisport and is the Executive Director of the Kyle Pease Foundation.

About the Pease Brothers

Together Kyle and Brent help other disabled athletes compete in the multisport & endurance world through their non-profit organization, The Kyle Pease Foundation. The Kyle Pease Foundation promotes success for young persons with disabilities by providing assistance to meet their individual needs through sports and competition. Programs include scholarship opportunities, adaptive sports equipment, and participating in educational campaigns around Cerebral Palsy.

The Pease brothers have completed over 40 races together since 2011. Brent and Kyle recently completed their second 140.6 mile race together at Ironman Florida with a time of 13 hours, 38 minutes. In 2013, the Pease brothers completed their first iron-distance race at Ironman, Wisconsin with a time of 15 hours, 9 minutes.

About Co-author Todd Civin

Todd Civin is a husband, father of five and grandfather of two to date. He is a graduate of Syracuse University Newhouse School of Public Communications. Civin is the founder and CEO of Civin Media Relations and is the Social Media Director for the Kyle Pease Foundation. He is the co-author of *One Letter at a Time* by Rick Hoyt and Todd Civin, *Destined to Run* by Wes Harding and Todd Civin and *Just My Game* by Jason Grilli and Todd Civin. He is overjoyed to add Kyle Pease's children's book, *Where There's a Wheel, There's a Way* to his resume.

About Illustrator Jason Boucher

Jason Boucher is an artist and mason. He has been in construction going on 16 years but has been an artist most of his life. He never took a lesson and is pretty much self-taught. He's married to his beautiful wife Erika and they have a beautiful daughter named Kayla and two handsome sons, Beau and Blake. It's his goal to be a full time illustrator and finally throw the work boots away!

On November 1, 2015, Kyle and Brent set out to complete the New York City Marathon. At mile 12, the back wheel on Kyle's running chair shattered, leaving the two unequipped to continue. Rather than giving up, Brent tied a rope to the axle of the chair where the tire used to roll and looped it around his shoulders. With the help of two strangers, they completed the remaining 14 miles, refusing to quit. On this day, Kyle and Brent proved that "Where is a No Wheel, There is Still a Way" ` A true lesson on perseverance. What follows is a poem written by blind, paraplegic poet, Laura Chagnon, commemorating the Pease Brothers' historic day.

The Will of Two Champions

By Laura Chagnon

The New York City Marathon, the Big Apple
Dreams and goals rising to the stars.

Brent and Kyle Pease
this team fueled by brotherly love
The vision of a finish line, a familiar friend.

An unpredictable journey, rolling the dice
where fate can hold the upper hand.
Unforeseen at mile 12, a broken wheel.

A dream slipping away
like mercury through a broken thermometer.
The desire of two champions, now being challenged.

Finding a way to persevere
resourcefulness, ingenuity and two angels.
The glow of the finish line beaming brighter.

Breaking the tape
fatigue and joy intertwined,
The sweet taste of accomplishment, pure elation!!!

Made in the USA
Columbia, SC
06 July 2019